Reptile Keeper's

Bearded Dragons

R. D. Bartlett
Patricia P. Bartlett

Acknowledgments

For shared knowledge and photographic opportunities, we extend our heartfelt appreciation to Karin Burns and Billy Griswold, hobbyists Liz Craig and Matthew Steen, Hester and the late Bert Langerwerf (Agama International), Bill and Kathy Love (Blue Chameleon Ventures), Buzz Ross, Peter and Phyllis Weis, and Rob MacInnes (Glades Herp).

Although our chart on medication was provided by Richard Funk, DVM, we also owe our sincerest thanks to Fredric Frye, DVM, for his comments on medications and other aspects of this manuscript.

Photo Credits

Billy Griswold: 19, 27, 34 (bottom); Shutterstock: i.
All other photos courtesy of Richard D. and Patricia P. Bartlett.

Cover Photos

Front cover; back cover; inside front cover, inside back cover: Shutterstock.

All inquiries should be addressed to:
Barron's Educational Series, Inc.
250 Wireless Boulevard
Hauppauge, NY 11788
www.barronseduc.com

ISBN-13: 978-0-7641-4094-5
ISBN-10: 0-7641-4094-9
Library of Congress Catalog Control Number: 2008939529

Printed in China
9 8 7 6 5 4 3 2 1

Contents

Preface

This book is designed to help you with the husbandry of one of today's most popular pet lizards, the bearded dragon, and, in particular, the inland bearded dragon. It includes husbandry and dietary information for these Australian omnivores. Bearded dragons are one of the easier lizards to provide for and are relatively confiding and responsive to their keepers. They have interesting territorial displays, attain a moderate size, and can be kept in relatively small quarters. If their basic needs are met, they can be easily captive bred for several seasons and will live for 7 to 10-plus years. Because virtually all dragons now available in the American pet trade are bred in captivity, you don't need to worry about any impact on wild populations.

Let us tell you a bit about us. We both kept reptiles as kids. Dick was a livestock buyer for a national chain store, owned a pet store, and worked as a cargo agent for a national airline before retiring. He wrote a column for *Reptiles* magazine for 15 years. Patti worked as an editor and writer for a publishing company before becoming a museum director. We began keeping and breeding reptiles in 1972 and since then have bred more than 200 species.

We hope that you will enjoy your bearded dragon, and that the information we have provided will make it just a little easier to understand and interact with your pet lizard.

Dick and Patti Bartlett
Gainesville, Florida, U.S.A.

Introduction

The bearded dragon is great pet lizard. It consumes a variety of foods you can buy in your grocery store. It is a calm lizard, and becomes tame readily if handled gently on a regular basis. It is large enough to pick up and hold, and small enough to be easily held in your hands or upon your arm. Beardeds are responsive creatures and soon equate the opening of their cage top with good news, such as being fed or being held. They often watch their owner's face as if interested in what the owner has to say. Bearded dragons are readily bred in captivity, which means none are taken from the wild for the pet market.

Although there are eight kinds of bearded dragons, the most popular is the inland bearded dragon, *Pogona vitticeps*. In these pages, we'll tell you all about the inland dragon and some of the other "beardies."

This inland bearded dragon is alert, looking up at its owner; its beard is partially distended.

What Is the Bearded Dragon?

The bearded dragons, named for the loose skin or beard under the throat, are heavy-bodied, attractive Australian lizards. They have a quiet and confiding nature and seem unafraid of and very responsive to their keepers.

All are in the genus *Pogona* (formerly *Amphibolurus*) in the family Agamidae. At least four of the eight species of these lizards are captive bred in some numbers. The most popular member of the genus is the inland bearded dragon, *P. vitticeps*, a large species, now captive bred by the thousands of specimens annually. This is the species about which most is known.

As a group, bearded dragons are arid-dwelling, heliothermic (sun-basking), heat-tolerant lizards. Body temperatures of basking lizards may exceed 100° F. When cold, dragons become inactive and will not feed. Although often seen on the ground, bearded dragons climb dead trees and other such low-elevation positions to bask and display. The most dominant males usually assume the highest positions. A curious arm-waving, called circumduction, is exhibited by both young and adults and apparently serves as a "I mean no harm" gesture. We have noted the gesture is used particularly often by subadult and adult female lizards.

The beards are used by both sexes as a part of the courtship and territorial displays, although the beards of the males are larger and usually much darker. Beards are darkest during breeding season. The beards are quickly displayed or distended and both sexes bob their heads as part of this display. Males bob more quickly than females. All bearded dragons are oviparous, laying eggs to reproduce. The smaller species are primarily insectivorous, but the larger forms are

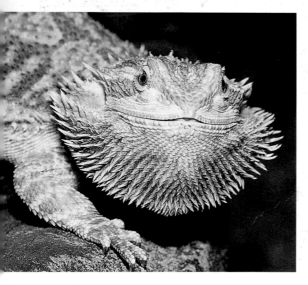

A male inland bearded is an impressive creature when he displays his beard.

quite omnivorous, feeding in the wild on vegetation such as dandelions and other flowers, beetles, and a variety of seeds.

Meet the Eight Bearded Dragons

The **inland bearded dragon**, *P. vitticeps*, is a spectacular lizard that has gone from comparative obscurity to ready pet shop availability in only a decade. In its native habitat, it is common over much of arid and semi-arid southeastern Australia. At an adult length of 18–22 in., it is marginally shorter than some other *Pogona* species, but it is more robust. In the wild, it is found amid eucalypti and acacias, in brushlands, on sandy and rocky plains, and amid short grasses. It may be seen basking and displaying from elevated rocks, tree trunks, and fence posts. Its ground color varies from tan to gray to brick red and usually blends well with the soils on which it is found. Broad, lighter lines and some degree of blotching on the back are usually present, although older males may be nearly unicolored. It is quite capable of moving rapidly but may depend on its cryptic appearance to evade detection.

Wayne Van Devender recently related to us his experiences in sighting a large inland dragon in New South Wales. The lizard darted away as it was approached and seemed to disappear. After a considerable search, the lizard was resighted. It was nearly invisible where it lay, hunched and with closed eyes, amidst a field of cow "patties."

The inland bearded's evolution as a desert lizard is revealed in its behavior when kept in a terrarium with proper heating and lighting choices. When it basks, its body temperature may exceed 100° F. It enjoys basking atop elevated limbs and rocks and will utilize a brightly lit basking area having a surface temperature of 110–115° F.

The classic inland bearded dragon—this one is a mixture of gray, tan, and white.

An inland bearded relative, the coastal bearded dragon (*P. barbata*) has a distinctive mustard-yellow lining to the mouth.

As with the other species of bearded dragons, the most dominant male usually assumes the most prominent position.

Young sexually mature inland dragon females can be amazingly prolific. In captivity, large, well-fed females may produce over 150 eggs a year (occasionally with more than 35 in a clutch).

Pogona barbata, the **coastal bearded dragon**, is not as popular or as readily available as the inland bearded, but captive-born stock is available. This is marginally the largest species. It may reach a length of 22 in., with just over half the length being tail. This is generally the species darkest in coloration, with some being almost charcoal in ground color. Other specimens may have a

ground color of buff or sand red. Enlarged conical spines adorn the beard of this species, making the breeding display especially impressive. The mouth is opened as part of the display, and the bright lemon to mustard lining is an impressive sight. Although coastal bearded dragons are occasionally available to hobbyists, they are considered a little more difficult to keep and breed than the inland bearded dragon.

Pogona barbata is found in wooded parts of eastern Australia. Near Sydney, during cooler weather, the coastal bearded has been found to overwinter in burrows beneath rocks. Because it is adapted to habitats along Australia's relatively humid east coast, the coastal bearded dragon might be the best choice for hobbyists located in humid areas. It is somewhat more arboreal than the other dragons, climbing and basking atop higher brush piles, leaning trees, fence posts, and similar vantage points. Its diet is the same as the inland bearded dragon.

Two small "beardless" bearded dragons complete the list of bearded dragon species currently available in American and European herpetoculture. The first, the (beardless) **dwarf bearded dragon**, *Pogona minor*, is less popular in America than in Europe. Its adult size is just over a foot in length. It occurs widely in the arid lands of Western Australia, western South Australia, and southwestern Northern Territory. The second beardless species is the **lesser bearded dragon**, *Pogona henrylawsoni*. It is second only to the inland bearded dragon in popularity, but this is not meant to indicate that it is common in collections. In size, the lesser bearded dragon may reach 14 in.

The dwarf bearded dragon, *Pogona minima*, lacks the chin beard, and is two-thirds the size of an inland bearded.

in length. (You may see this lizard listed under two erroneous names, *P. rankeni* and *P. brevis*. The common name of Lawson's dragon is also often applied.)

The lesser bearded dragon comes from central Queensland, Australia. It has been hybridized with the inland bearded dragon, and the young are marketed as vittikens dragons, and are occasionally provided the erroneous and invalid name of *Pogona vittikens* on dealers' price lists.

The four remaining kinds of bearded dragons are all quietly colored in sandy hues, and most have prominent dorsal banding and/or blotching. The patterns are often brightest on juveniles of both sexes and adult females.

The **western bearded dragon** is scientifically known as *Pogona minima*, and it is captive bred in the United States and Europe in small numbers. It is still considered a race of the dwarf bearded dragon, *P. minor*, by some authorities. The western bearded is a 13-in. long dragon, found in a very restricted area of the western part of Western Australia. It has a well-defined row of lateral spines and enlarged head spines of disparate sizes.

Lawson's dragon, or the lesser bearded dragon, is slightly smaller than the inland bearded dragon. It looks very much like its popular cousin but is only rarely offered for sale.

The **small-scaled dragon**, *Pogona microlepidota*, is one of the less spiny of this genus of very spiny lizards. It is one of the larger species, attaining an overall length of about 18 in., and is found in a small area of coastal northern Western Australia. It lacks prominent nuchal spines and enlarged spines in the center of the throat. As far as we know, no specimens of the small-scaled dragon or of the following two species have been reported in the United States.

Mitchell's dragon, *Pogona mitchelli*, is a 14-in.-long species that inhabits the more arid northern regions of Western Australia and adjacent Northern Territory. It was long considered a race of *P. minor*, the dwarf bearded dragon. Mitchell's dragon tends to have a large, orangish head and two clusters of nuchal spines.

The fourth species, *Pogona nullarbor*, is referred to as the **Nullarbor Plain bearded dragon**. It occurs in the arid Nullabor Plains region in southeastern Western Australia and adjacent South Australia. It is adult at about 13 in. in total length and lacks clusters of nuchal spines. Its head is not as noticeably broadened as some other species, and it lacks noticeably enlarged gular (chin) spines.

Longevity

Although the life spans of the various dragons are virtually unreported on in the wild, those of captives are somewhat better known. Compared to some lizards, the bearded dragons do not seem particularly long-lived. Many accounts exist, for both the small and large dragon species, of longevity only in the 5- to 6-year range.

A coastal bearded dragon, wild-collected as an adult, lived as a captive for 9 years and 11 months. And with a known maximum age of 10 years and 1 month, the inland bearded dragon is marginally the longest lived.

The lack of a beard is evident in this young *P. henrylawsoni*—but these are still appealing lizards, with much the same behavioral characteristics of their larger cousin.

The Bearded Dragon as a Pet

Choosing a Healthy Bearded Dragon

When you select your bearded dragon, choose a specimen that is lively and alert. If at all possible, choose one that seems unafraid of being handled. Although there isn't much difference in personality between the males and females, the males are by nature more outgoing than the females.

A few words about buying baby dragons and why size does matter: The smallest dragon you should consider buying should be at least 6 in. in length or 6 weeks old. Babies smaller than 6 in. are just out of the egg and may not have fed. (Some hatchlings will not eat anything and are termed non-feeders. They die of starvation and who knows what else. Non-feeders are exasperating/expensive/frustrating at the very least and a waste of a reptile life.)

Whether you're buying a 6-in. normal bearded for $50 or a 6-in. translucent for $400, you need to have things stacked in your favor for the animal's long life. Buy an animal that feeds; it isn't rude to ask to see your potential pet feed before you buy it.

Certainly baby dragons are cute little things, but a baby isn't for everyone. Keep in mind that babies don't achieve their final adult coloration until they are 2 years old. Until then, with each successive shed, the final color gradually appears. Unless you know your dragon colors very well, you're going to have to trust your dealer when it comes to lineage and color prediction. Since prices for 6-in. babies of normal coloration start at $35 and zip up to $400-plus for the more unusual colors, one could easily be led astray by an opportunistic (we won't imply "unscrupulous") seller.

Many people want an older dragon. If sex matters to you, buy a yearling. If you want to buy a specific color and you're not certain you can trust the breeder/seller, wait and buy a yearling or a two year old. You'll be able to see for yourself what you're getting. If you just plain want a bearded and don't care about the color or the age or the sex, consider contacting a rescue operation and adopting one of their rescues. You'll have to pay the adoption fee,

Inland bearded lizards tame down very well and will rest in apparent contentment on your arm or hand.

The vent and the underside of the hind legs of the female bearded dragon (left) are unadorned. The vent of the male (right) conceals the subtle bulge of the hemipenes (male sex organs) while the underside of the hind legs bear femoral and preanal pores. The pores emit a waxy substance that leaves a scent trail when the male crawls across solid objects.

but you'll know you're helping a creature that has never had any control whatsoever over its life circumstances. That has to count for something.

Handling Your Dragon

Providing it is done gently, inland bearded dragons quickly become tolerant of handling. Adults are more tolerant than juveniles. Despite their being much easier to handle than many other lizards, it is still a good idea to restrain bearded dragons when you are holding them outdoors. Even when lying quietly on your shoulder or arm, if startled, a dragon will drop to the ground and scamper rapidly away. If allowed to fall for more than a short distance, injury can occur. When lifting a dragon, support it adequately, encircling its body with your hand and allowing it to hold your fingers with its claws.

Sexing Your Dragon

Even experienced breeders cannot sex a baby bearded dragon accurately. If you buy a baby, and if the sex is important

to you, ask your supplier if you can exchange the animal if it turns out not to be the sex you wanted. If you're buying an adult bearded, the sexing process is somewhat easier if you have several to look at.

Male adult dragons have a wider tail base. When the cloacal opening is exposed by pulling back the skin around the vent, the cloacal opening for the males is wider than for the females. Males have a broader, more strongly triangular head than the females. When gravid, the basic body shape of the female is heavier than that of the male. Displaying males have a darker beard (especially during the breeding season). The femoral and preanal pores of the males—the pores on the underside of each hind leg and anterior to the vent—are darker and larger than the femoral pores of the females. Males have more aggressive behavior during the breeding season, which means that they more readily flare out their beards and open their mouths when you open the cage. (This display is meant to intimidate other beardeds and does not mean the bearded will bite. In a way, it's a compliment.) Females often use circumduction rather than beard displays.

Hemipenes of both juveniles and adult males can be "popped," or rolled out using pressure from your thumb, but this can be injurious to the lizards. We strongly urge that this be done only by those experienced in the technique.

Obtaining Your Bearded Dragon

Depending on their color, bearded dragons can vary in purchase price from relatively inexpensive (less than $75) to quite expensive (several hundred dollars). Those offered most frequently by pet stores are usually a generic tan to brown in color. Because the brilliantly colored morphs—red-headed, gold-headed, sandfire, etc.—are considerably more expensive, you may need to special-order through your local pet store or go online to find a specialty dealer/breeder. The special color morphs can also be found at reptile expos.

Whatever color you select, remember that all dragons have the same needs. Your bearded is a living, thinking creature and deserves the best care you can give it throughout its life. Should circumstances change and the care of your bearded is more than you can provide, live up to your responsibility. Contact one of the bearded rescue organizations (*beardeddragon.org* is one).

Pet Stores

If given even modest care, bearded dragons will easily withstand the rigors of pet store life, and there certainly could hardly be anything more convenient than the acquisition of your dragon from a local source. We advocate shopping at pet stores because of the convenience and because ideally, you can discuss your potential purchase, one-on-one, with a knowledgable store employee. Such things as routine care are easily covered. You will be the best judge of the quality of animals and care information provided by a local store.

But there are some things that your pet store cannot be expected to know. Among others are the actual origins, or genetics, of a given specimen. Remember that your local pet shop is often two or even three or four times removed from the breeder. The employee can only repeat what he or she has been told by the supplier.

Reptile and Amphibian Expos

Herp expos began on a regional basis about 20 years ago. With the increasing popularity of reptiles as pets and the ready supply of captive-bred reptiles, expos have become good sources for reptile purchase.

An expo is merely the commercial gathering of dealers, breeders, and hobbyists, all under one roof. The expo may vary in size from the 650-plus tables of the National Reptile Breeders' Expo in Daytona, Florida, every August to others that are much smaller but almost as comprehensive. Bearded dragons, in a variety of color morphs and prices, are available at nearly every expo.

Breeders

Breeders can be spare-room hobbyists who produce only a few clutches of bearded dragons annually to commercial breeders who produce literally

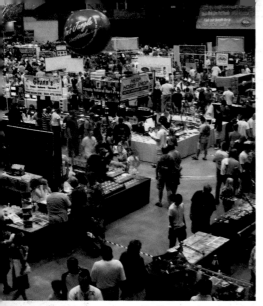

Reptile expos are good places to buy bearded dragons, from standard (inexpensive) to very pretty (expensive!). You are usually talking directly to the breeder at an expo.

Reptile Dealers

The continuing popularity of reptiles has allowed the development of reptile dealers. Besides breeding fair numbers of the reptiles they offer, reptile dealers deal directly with other breeders (across the world) and may even be direct importers. If you want one of the rarer kinds of bearded, you may need to talk to a reptile dealer. Many such dealers both buy and sell reptiles and amphibians at herp expos.

Online Purchase and Shipping

If you do order a dragon from an online source, your dragon will be shipped to you. Shipping used to be a complex process, including checking air bill numbers and flight times and finally driving to the nearest airport to pick up your shipment. Now lizards can legally be shipped to you via FedEx or the United States Postal Service. It's that simple. There are packing regulations, but they are for the animal's benefit and they aren't complex.

The individual or company you order your bearded from will be very familiar with the different services. Just be certain to order the fastest service (something the USPS cannot always promise). Being shipped is stressful to any animal. Packages get left on a loading dock or sit in an unheated (or uncooled) delivery truck for hours at a time. If the animal is shipped USPS, you will probably have to drive to your local post office during their normal working hours to pick up the shipment (which means forget about picking it up on a weekend). Some shippers guarantee live delivery. Getting a replacement lizard at no charge is nice, but we hasten to point out that if your animal dies in transit, it's one animal life wasted.

thousands of hatchlings. With each passing year, more and more breeders present the fruits of their labors at herp expos, but there are many who prefer to sell in other ways. Refer to the classified or display ads in specialty reptile and amphibian magazines (see the Special Interest Groups section, page 42), the classified ads in your local paper, or go online (try *kingsnake.com*). Breeders, especially one living near you, can offer healthy, well-acclimated baby dragons, as well as an occasional adult and accurate husbandry information. They keep records of genetics, lineage, fecundity, health, and quirks of the individual lizards with which they work.

Some breeders concentrate on breeding large numbers of normal colored dragons for the pet trade. Others produce normal colored pet trade dragons and also selectively breed for enhanced colors and patterns.

Your shipper may also be able to use UPS. Our local UPS office has told us they cannot accept live animal shipments knowingly, yet an acquaintance of ours in the southern part of Florida uses UPS for all his animal shipments and the shipments are clearly marked "live reptiles." Call your local UPS office and ask.

All bearded shipments should be marked "Live Harmless Lizards." A reputable breeder/dealer/individual will not lie to a carrier (a shipping company) about what is being shipped. Beside being dishonest (and unfair to the animal being shipped), not marking a package accurately could provoke a carrier into refusing all reptile shipments.

If you have any questions about what may or may not be shipped, call your local shipping company.

Payment

The price you are quoted for your lizards is just that—only for the animals themselves. Shipping charges will be extra. The method of payment should be agreed upon and fully understood by both you, the purchaser, and the shipper at the time of ordering. Generally speaking, shipping will cost you about $30. Unless the shipper knows you well, he or she will almost always insist your bearded be paid for in full (including boxing charges, a fee for the actual shipping container) prior to shipment. This may be done with a credit card, money order, or a cashier's check. Most shippers will accept personal checks but will not ship until the check has cleared their bank (usually a week or so after deposit).

The difference between the Red flame (top) and a Sandfire (bottom) bearded are evident when the two are compared.

Colors

The Colors of the Inland Bearded Dragon

In appearance, hatchlings of all the color phases mentioned here are very similar. It is not until they are more than one-third grown that coloration begins to brighten. Adult males tend to be brighter in general coloration and/or less well patterned than females. Additionally, a given dragon may vary significantly in color according to temperature and mood. Dragons are usually at their most brilliant when at optimal body temperature, dominant, and displaying, but they may also be quite brightly colored when sleeping soundly after darkness. Some females may have black(ish) beards, but there is

usually white scale-tipping, whereas the beards of the males are dark overall. Dragons of both sexes darken beard colors when displaying and at other times of peak alertness.

Normal

This morph has a variable ground color of tan, brownish, grayish, or, more rarely, olive green. The face is banded, and the dorsolateral markings are lighter.

Selective breeding for specific colors or color combinations has created some gorgeous beardeds.

The earliest breeders made up their own names for their color lines. Sandfire Ranch, the first commercial breeder of beardeds to our knowledge, bred for red and yellow lines, creating the Sandfire red and Sandfire gold. When these two colors were bred together, the offspring were labeled Sandfire redxSandfire gold. Dragon's Den stepped up to the breeding plate and produced a yellow line, the Sunburst line, and a red line, the Bloods. They were one of the first to breed and market leucistic Snows. Weis Reptiles bred for a red line, the Red Flames. Peter Weis' Red Flame line produced beardeds with prominent

Inland bearded dragons are at their brightest when they are warm. This Sandfire morph relaxes on a side display table at a breeders' expo in Daytona, Florida.

facial markings, a ground color of orange-tan to buff, and orange to orange-red side blotches; the angle of the mouth was often bright orange. Weis dropped out of the market while Sandfire and Dragon's Den remain.

Selective breeding has also created big beardeds, about a quarter to a third larger than the usual inland bearded dragons. The German giants, as they were called, were interbred with color morphs to create big, bright-bearded dragons.

When buying a colored bearded, unless you buy directly from one of the originators of a color line, odds are better than even you are probably buying one of mixed parentage from those original breeders.

Breeders-come-latelies, meaning those who were not in on the early days of breeding beardeds for color, have named their own descendant lines. That's why you'll see Peach, Salmon, Sunglow, Citrus, etc., lines, and you may hear some breeders swear they developed the line they are now selling. Ask them where they got their initial breeding stock.

If you're planning on breeding your beardeds, do check their parentage. Avoid breeding two that are closely related. Inbred baby beardeds tend to be small, runty in appearance (just like a runt in a dog litter—smaller, poor conformation, more likely to have bone defects), may have kinked tails, and have a high incidence of non-feeding.

Other Color Characteristics

Leucistic, developed in the early 2000s. This is a white body coloration with dark eyes (leucistic means literally "white-like"). This is an actual color, whereas albinism is lack of color. (A

The term "orange tiger" is used to describe a dragon with a yellow to orange body with darker, strongly contrasting lateral bands.

few albino beardeds have been hatched, but the survival rate is dismal and they remain extremely uncommon.) Clear toe nails indicate the animal is leucistic—this is one of the early markers for this characteristic, so you do not have to wait two years to see adult coloration. If not all of the toenails are clear, the animal is not a pure leucistic.

The *hypo* color line produces beardeds with reduced black pigment (when used to describe color, hypo means "under" or "beneath"). This is a brighter lizard. Brown blotches will be a pale tan to yellow, and a tan background will be yellow. Other colors can be bred into a hypo line to brighten the added color.

Het is short for heterozygous, meaning a recessive gene for the next color mentioned. "Het for leucistic" means the lizard bears the recessive gene for that quality. You cannot tell from appearances if a bearded is heterozygous, because that quality is masked by the dominant gene. If you breed two hets together for leucistic, half of the young would be het leucistics, one quarter would be leucistic, and the final quarter of the clutch would be normal color. Punnet squares are used to determine the outcome of dominant and recessive genes. A Punnet square for heterozygous leucistic demonstrates that there is one dominant (N) and one recessive (n) gene contributed by each parent, like this:

	N	n
N	NN	Nn
n	Nn	nn

Eight-month-old Red flame and Sandfire dragons.

If you want to be certain of your bearded dragon's lineage, ask the breeder when he (or she) got the original breeding stock.

The Name Game

Using interesting names to help market reptiles is not new. It harkens back to the wild and wooly 1960s, before rules and restrictions brought an "anything-goes" business largely into line. Illegal stuff always brought a premium price and shipment inspections were rare, so it was worth the risk to bring in something from Australia, or something protected. Mislabeling was rampant, with black-headed pythons labeled boa constrictors. Since ID was never required to pick up a shipment, importers would use false names ("Bob Jones" was a popular choice) when bringing in a shipment, just in case there was something illegal in the shipment and the shipment was inspected.

Making up names for reptiles was not illegal and it was almost as much fun as importing. Importers would bring in a shipment of lizards listed as "ameivas." If the ameivas didn't sell the first week on the importer's mimeographed price list, they were listed as "emerald jungle runners" on the next price list. Whatever had not sold by the end of the next week became "canopy divers." Often the importer would add a personal note on creatures that needed a selling boost ("best I've ever seen" was a well-used phrase, certain to elicit a buying response from someone who didn't know better).

Pastel dragons have an orange-red head and a grayish-blue or grayish-pink body, legs, and tail.

Translucent dragons have skin with little pigment in the top layer. This imparts a curious sort of gray tinge to the body, until you look more closely.

Caging for Your Dragons

Bearded dragons are arid-land to semi-arid-land lizards. Most are primarily terrestrial, but they will climb any elevated vantage point. From these king-of-the-mountain positions, males and females thermoregulate and indulge in territorial and other displays. Although dragons are often thought of as indoor pets, where climatic conditions are arid and warm enough, they will thrive in outside cages. You may want to consider using outdoor caging during the summer months and switching to indoor caging during the cooler months.

Whether indoors or out, the size of the dragon cage should vary according to the sizes and number of the dragons kept therein. For a trio of adult inland bearded dragons, one male and two females, we suggest a cage with a floor that measures at least 1.5 ft. by 4 ft. This floor is about the same size as that of a 50-gallon aquarium. A larger terrarium would be even better. From one to three dwarf bearded dragons could be successfully housed in a 30-gallon tank (with a 1.5 ft. by 3 ft. floor), but they would utilize a far larger tank were it to be provided.

A dragon cage does not need to be elaborate but it does need to provide room, warmth, hiding and basking spaces, as well as space for food and water dishes. Your dragons may not drink from the water dish, so mist their heads with water each morning.

Substrate can be dirt from your yard, play sand, shredded hardwood, chipped kenaf stems, or even one of the commercial clay mixtures for digging.

A larger colony of dragons would require additional floor space.

It might seem that baby or immature dragons could be kept in a smaller tank than the adults, but because baby dragons tend to be more aggressive toward their cage mates than the adults are, allowing proportionately more cage space would be even better for the juveniles. Baby dragons can and will bite off each others' toes and tailtips.

When kept colonially, adult dragons become territorial and establish a hiearchy. Once males have become sexually mature, it is usually not possible to keep more than one to a cage. Females will also work out a pattern of dominance, and the most dominant specimen may become persistently aggressive toward any other females. You may need to provide separate caging.

Substrates

Despite the conventional wisdom that sand is an unsatisfactory substrate for bearded dragons, we have used smooth (not sharp silica) sand as a substrate for desert lizards for years without mishap. We recommend a sand substrate for any naturalistic terrarium. Although some hobbyists have voiced concern about using sand, citing intestinal impaction, in over 40 years of lizard keeping, we've never had an incidence of this occur.

You can buy a ready-made substrate for your beardeds at your pet store or online. Three of the more recommended are ground walnut shell, chipped kenaf stems (a hibiscus relative), or shredded hardwood pulp. These granular substrates are absorbent and make it easy to scoop out dragon waste or any spilled liquid. One of the newer substrates is bird seed (honest!). It won't clog up your bearded's digestive system if it is swallowed and it is fun to dig in (but there's no way a bearded can make a burrow). Other substrates might be newspaper or Kraft paper (neither provides good traction), Astroturf, or indoor/outdoor carpeting. No matter the substrate, it must be kept scrupulously clean.

Part of what you want to avoid in bearded caging is any substrate that will stay too moist. This means no shredded coconut fiber, chipped bark, or recycled paper twists. We suggest sand or even flat sheets of newspaper.

Window Cages

To allow hobbyists to make sunlight available to their herps, a "window cage" that slides in and out of an opened window on extendable tracks has been developed. This should prove a real boon to apartment, condo, or city dwellers who would be otherwise unable to allow their lizards access to natural sunlight.

Rather than purchase a window cage, you may choose to build a less sophisticated, but suitably sized cage of wood and wire or of wire panels J-clamped together. This homemade cage can be hooked or wedged into a window. Although less convenient than a cage on tracks, it will more than suffice.

When using a window cage, monitor the heat buildup, and always provide a cooler shaded area to which your lizards can retreat if they choose.

The Arid-land Terrarium

Bearded dragons will thrive either in desert or savanna terraria. Properly arranged arid lands provide attractive habitats that stimulate both the interest of the hobbyist and the normal and social behaviors of the beardeds.

Cage Furniture

Rock ledges and caves, individual basking rocks, potted arid-land plants (including dried grasses), corkbark hiding areas, and cholla cactus skeletons can be provided both for decoration and the psychological well being of your specimen(s). To promote low humidity, the terrarium should be in a well-ventilated area, and the top should be covered with a screen.

Use heat lamps and full spectrum lights when keeping dragons indoors.

Make arrangements for UVA/UVB lighting over the basking spot.

How to Set Up a Naturalistic Arid-land Terrarium

Choose a tank of suitable and adequate size. Be certain that the stand on which the terrarium will be placed can safely hold the weight.

Materials Needed

- Terrarium and stand

- Aquarium sealant to affix rock and limbs if necessary

- Sand substrate

- Small pots of drought-tolerant succulents like sanseveria or pachypodium

- 2-in.-thick Styrofoam insert, of preferred size (dried grasses will be inserted into this)

- Phillips screwdriver or icepick to make holes (in which the grasses will stand) in Styrofoam insert

- Rocks and/or other terrarium furniture (rocks, contorted grape and manzanita branches, cholla skeletons, corkbark [both flat and tubular sections], water receptacle) and camouflaged hide boxes

- Undertank heater(s)

- Terrarium top (metal-framed screen or wire top is best; full glass tops are not acceptable)

- Lighting fixtures and bulbs (full spectrum fluorescent and heat-producing, directed-beam, color-corrected incandescent bulbs)

- Small ventilation fan (optional)

Setup Procedure

1. Place the tank on its stand with the undertank heater in place at one end of the tank (follow directions carefully when placing and connecting the heaters).
2. If you want to add dried grasses as part of your decor, use the screwdriver to poke holes into the styrofoam, and insert the dried grasses into the holes. Put the styrofoam in place in the tank (you'll pour the sand around the insert later).
3. Position and seal in place any heavy cage furniture (rocks, limbs, etc.). This is a particularly important step, for if these items are just laid atop the surface sand, your dragons may burrow under them, and the rocks may settle on them. You may need to provide two basking rocks if you are keeping more than one bearded. Allow a minimum of 24 hours for sealant curing.
4. Pour the fine sand into the tank to the desired depth, carefully covering the styrofoam insert (taking care not to break the grasses—the dragons will do this soon enough!). Again, we suggest a depth of several inches.
5. Position the plants. We prefer to leave the plants in their pots and sink the pots to the rim in the sand. This contains the moisture (and plant food) better when the plants are watered and prevents extensive areas of sand from becoming overly moist or saturated with fertilizer. If the plants begin suffering from insufficient light or other growth problems, replacing them is a simple matter. Alternatively, the plants can be removed from their pots and planted directly in the sand. Extreme care will then need to be used in watering and fertilizing, and replacing the plants is more difficult.

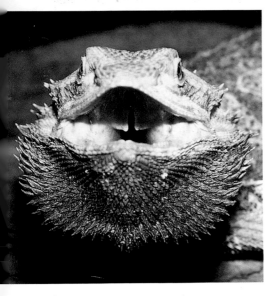

A warmed dragon exposed to natural sunlight may give its owner a "back off!" message when approached.

Dragons will readily climb tree trunks or rock piles to obtain the best sunning spot—and the uppermost dragon is usually the dominant dragon.

6. Arrange the water bowl and any remaining lightweight cage furniture either on the sand surface or partially buried, as desired. Depending on the number and compatibility of the bearded to be kept in the tank, from one to several secure hide boxes/hiding areas should be included.
7. Position and affix the lighting fixtures over the basking rocks.
8. Plan to do some routine maintenance on the tank as a matter of course. For example, you will need to scoop the sand away from the styrofoam insert and replace the dried grasses as they are broken by the dragons. The plants will also need to be replaced occasionally.

Lighting and Heating

Bulbs that induce plant growth should be used for planted desert terraria. The directed beams of these can also provide sand-surface thermal gradients. Warmth can also be provided by using an undertank heater. Provide the desired thermal gradient by heating only one end of the terrarium and use a UVA/UVB light. These lights enable your bearded to metabolize the calcium in its diet. A heated end temperature of about 92–100° F will be fine. The cool end should be 80–85° F.

Outdoor Cages

Predators and Fire Ants

Predators can be a problem for outdoor caging. Some animals, such as raccoons, opossums, and domestic dogs may destroy screen barriers to get at either your lizards or your lizards' food. Feral rats and mice may chew through barriers. Even if actual predation on your beardeds does not occur, cage destruction can result in your pets escaping. Hawks, owls, crows, roadrunners, shrikes, and even grackles may prey on specimens in open-topped cages. Netting covers preclude this possibility. Burrowing mammals such as shrews, voles, and moles may enter a cage from beneath and prey upon hibernating, or otherwise quiescent, beardeds or on clutches of eggs or newly emerging babies. Burying your cage 8- to 12-in. deep will usually protect your animals from these subterranean species. Take all necessary steps to preclude predation when—not after—building your outside cages.

Ants, and especially fire ants, are among the more serious lizard predators, and their exclusion is not only often initially overlooked but also downright difficult. These insects can quickly and efficiently ravage a bearded, leaving behind dead and dying lizards. When situating your outdoor cage, avoid ant-prone areas of your yard, and immediately combat any indication of ant infiltration.

Outdoor Ring Cages

Ring cages are made from a length of 3-ft.-high aluminum sheeting sunk one foot into the ground. They are circular and can be of any diameter, but we found that an 8- to 10-ft. diameter is ideal. Ring cages are relatively inexpensive.

The easiest way to outline and sink the sheeting is to use a post-hole digger attached to a 4.5-ft. length of twine. The other end of the twine is noosed loosely around a post tapped into the ground where the center of the cage is to be. By keeping the posthole digger at the outer limit of the twine, it is a relatively simple matter to dig the foot-deep trench needed for the aluminum.

No footer is needed for these cages. The aluminum sheeting is then set into the trench and leveled (this can be painstaking), and the two ends are riveted together. The trench is filled on both sides, with particular care being given to the inside perimeter. After the trench is filled, the cage is essentially done. Hiding places/hibernacula of small diameter terra cotta drainage pipes can then be slanted into the ground, and several elevated perching areas of stones, logs, or other furniture added. Be certain that your dragons cannot leap from atop the cage furniture to the top of the ring and escape. Remember that after having basked in natural, unfiltered sunlight, a reptile is often more alert and agile than one kept indoors, even if you have provided ultraviolet light.

Plants for Indoor and Outdoor Cages

To have the very best naturalistic terraria, it is necessary to pay as much attention to the selection of your plants as to your selection of animals. For indoor caging, remember that the nearer the tip of a leaf is to an incandescent lightbulb, the more light and warmth are present. Thus, although the top of a sansevieria leaf may be receiving sufficient light for proper growth, the leaf may be severely burned by the heat from the bulb. Choose and position plants and bulbs sympathetically. Be ready to change plant species from those requiring high light situations to species less demanding if growth becomes spindly or discolored.

Caging should provide a prime basking spot for each bearded.

Many garden departments of home improvement stores stock a variety of cactus. Select those that are sturdy, spineless, and lack rigid branches or leaves that can be easily broken.

Cacti

Many species and cultivars of common and easily grown cacti are available at stores and nurseries. Most grow well under intense artificial lighting, and some flower freely under such conditions. Despite their obvious armament, we have used cacti in our terraria over the decades and have never had any problems. Among others that grow well are the genus *Mammillaria*; several of the less lethally armed fishhook cacti, *Ferocactus*; star cacti, *Astrophytum*; and the comparatively spineless beaver-tail cacti, which are cultivars of the genus *Opuntia*.

Haworthias and Gasterias

These commonly grown nursery plants cluster readily into impressive, dwarfed thickets. Most of these lily relatives have leaves tipped with a rather weak spine and weakly serrate, spiny leaf edges. Of the two genera, the haworthias seem the easier to cultivate and require little in the way of winter cooling. Most of the haworthias thrive amid the rocks in an arid-land terrarium. Some have comparatively tender leaves, whereas the leaves of others are tough and almost indestructible. These plants have rosettes of leaves and may be either a squat, rather broadly opened rosette or rather tall with the leaves clasping the stem. The gasterias, on the other hand, enjoy cooler and drier conditions during the short days of winter. Most of the commonly offered species in both genera will grow well in somewhat less light than most cacti.

Sansevierias

The many species and cultivars of snakeplant or mother-in-law-tongue (genus *Sansevieria*) are ideal for brilliantly lighted savanna tanks. These African plants have been naturalized in many other areas of the world. Many are popular houseplants.

Although agaves may seem an improbable choice, young agaves are tough plants that grow very slowly.

sansevierias are available in both normal and variegated forms.

There are species that have interesting cylindrical leaves, others that have curious spatulate leaves, and yet others that, while having normal leaves, form short ground-hugging rosettes. Those with which most of us are familiar have sturdy straplike leaves from 8 to 36 in. in height. The sansevierias are both hardy and drought tolerant. They can be propagated by offsets, by rooting leaf cuttings, and, more rarely, by seed. As would be expected, the plants need more water during their periods of active growth than when they are dormant. For those enthusiasts who like a little variety in terrarium plants, many of the

Pachypodiums

Smaller species of *Pachypodium*, spiny succulents from Africa and Madagascar, adapt well to the savanna terrarium. Sadly, *Pachypodium lamerei*, the species most often grown in pots, attains treelike proportions. The smallest species, *Pachypodium brevicaule*, is a cactiform species that is a remarkable rock-mimic with sparse leaves but beautiful yellow flowers. Between these are several ideal species of moderate size, differing structure, and superb hardiness, including *Pachypodium bispinosum* and *Pachypodium succulentum*.

Oddballs

Calibanus hookeri is a strange Mexican caudiciform (the ecological equivalent of cactus) plant that has numerous discrete tufts of raspy surfaced grassy leaves emerging from the caudex. It is hardy and ideal for the savanna terrarium.

Purslane or portulaca is sold by nurseries for both hanging garden baskets and as bedding plants. They are drought-tolerant succulents that are fragile and require very bright lighting. Because they are inexpensive and bear beautiful blossoms, these plants are occasionally used as expendable terrarium plants. Tortoises and herbivorous lizards readily eat both the foliage and blossoms.

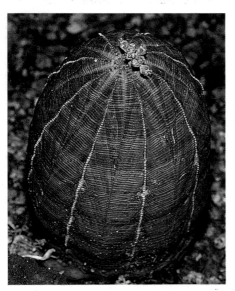

Euphorbias are the Old World equivalent of cactus. This global euphorbia would be a good choice for a bearded cage.

Feeding

Bearded dragons are omnivorous lizards. In nature, these lizards eat insects and snails (apparently from 40 to 75 percent of their diet is animal protein), berries and other available fruits, and some greenery. In captivity, dragons eat mealworms, giant mealworms, crickets, a variety of fruits, and finely chopped greens and vegetables of many kinds. Baby beardeds eat insects such as crickets, and they need a lot of them. Many breeders feed babies twice daily. Chopped greens (mustard, collard, beet), a little escarole, kale, and green cabbage are all good and nourishing food items. Chopped, fully thawed, frozen mixed vegetables and very little chopped fruit can also be given. (A food processor works wonders in the preparation of these foods.) The leaves and blossoms of dandelions and nasturtiums are also fine food items as would be a very occasional pre-killed pinky (or just weaned) mouse.

Freeze-dried, canned and prepared bearded dragon food is now available. Some of these preparations are touted as "complete diets," but we suggest that you augment them with fresh veggies and some insects. Go for dietary variety rather than dietary convenience when planning a bearded dragon's diet.

Note: Because of the calcium-binding oxalic acid they contain, do not feed spinach or related plants (see the Health section for more details on the importance of calcium levels).

Dragon's Diet

Veggies (finely chopped)	Animal protein
Mustard greens	Gray crickets (*Acheta*)
Collard greens	Giant mealworms (*Zophobas*)
Beet greens	Mealworms (*Tenebrio*)
Kale	Waxworms (*Galleria*), sparingly
Bok choy	Pinky mice (*Mus*), occasionally
Thawed mixed vegetables	Roaches (several genera) either captive raised
Fancy dark lettuces (not iceberg)	or from an insecticide-free area
Sprouts (bean and alfalfa)	
Green beans	
Peas (snow and other)	
Nasturtium leaves and flowers	
Hibiscus leaves and flowers	
Dandelion leaves and flowers	

Silkworms are a good food source, and you can easily raise them, feeding them powdered food you cook in a microwave.

Some dragons may opt to eat only a few favored items out of their daily offerings. This can be as unsatisfactory as simply offering a single item at each meal. Preferential selection becomes difficult when the veggies are finely chopped or mixed in a food processor. We should insist that our charges eat a healthy diet, all the while skewing dietary offerings toward what would be normal for them.

Although bearded dragons, and especially the babies, will gulp down and consume large food items like bigger beetles and chunks of fruit, big food items are not good for these lizards. Once in the stomach, items larger than ¼ the dragon's head can cause the dragon to experience tetanic

Mealworms can be purchased in lots of 50 to 1000, and can be fed a mixture of oats and greens so they provide a nutritious food.

shock, tremors, and hind leg paralysis and can result in death.

Some breeders and keepers suggest that hatchling dragons not be fed veggies, but we feel that vegetables should be offered from the very first feeding. In this way, the dragons become used to greens and accept them readily throughout their life.

There is speculation that if fed in large amounts and over long periods, high-fat items—such as pinky and freshly weaned mice—may be harmful to the health of insectivorous or omnivorous lizards. It is always better to feed a varied natural or a quasi-natural diet to any captive reptile or amphibian, with bearded dragons being no exception. Mice, an unnatural, high-fat food as far as bearded dragons are concerned, should be offered only sparingly. Pinkies are useful as a food item to help female dragons regain lost weight after they lay their eggs.

The Role of Natural, Unfiltered Sunlight in Calcium Utilization

Natural, unfiltered sunlight unquestionably provides the best possible lighting (and heat) for bearded dragons. Many of us do not have access to natural sunlight for our beardeds, but we can provide a close substitute, and that is lighting that emits both UVA and UVB light. Read labels very carefully. When selecting lighting, insist on a light that gives off both UVA and UVB lighting. Both are essential for your beardie—UVA for natural behavior, UVB for calcium metabolism.

To put it modestly, not all lighting is worth your money. As you read the labels on reptile lighting, you will discover deceptive wording, careful omissions, and blatant lies. It's a little bit like online dating—what gets omitted from a description is as important as what is stated.

In a nutshell, buy only a light that promises both UVA and UVB lighting. Lights that claim to be "full spectrum," "reptile lighting," "reptile sun," "daylight," "day," "reptile glo," and "basking" are NOT what you want for your beardeds. Do not believe any salesperson who assures you that these lights will do just fine. These lights may provide UVA, but they cannot give your bearded UVB.

Without UVB, your bearded cannot use the calcium in his food. Without calcium for his bones and in his blood, your bearded is headed for a devastating metabolic bone disease (called simply "MBD") that will warp his skeleton, should he live. Metabolic bone disease is entirely preventable but not entirely reversible. A good diet and UVA/UVB lighting are critical.

UVA/UVB lights come in two forms. One is a big incandescent light bulb that looks like a flood light. It puts out an amazing amount of heat, which will suit your beardeds just fine. These bulbs cost about $50 each and the big porcelain clamp lamp needed will cost another $15.

UVA/UVB lights can also be purchased as fluorescent lights, but read the label carefully. There are several types of fluorescent UVA/UVB bulbs. The high-UVB types cost about $30 a bulb. None of them requires a special lighting fixture. The very real disadvantage to the fluorescent lights is the steadily decreasing amount of UVA/UVB emitted. The lights will light up, but after six months, they give off no UVA/UVB. Using these lights

Chopped vegetables from your grocery store are part of a healthy diet for bearded dragons.

longer than six months is like watering down baby formula. You penalize those you want most to take care of. Can you remember (and will you act?) to replace a light that still lights up? At least the incandescent light burns out and you know it must be replaced. We don't trust the fluorescent lights ourselves—and we enjoy watching a bearded waddle over to his basking perch when we approach the tank to turn on the incandescent UVA/UVB light. (In a related aside, we have found that some snakes and lizards that are reluctant feeders in captivity become ready feeders when UVA/UVB lighting is added to their cages.)

Vitamin–Mineral Supplements

Vitamin–mineral supplements—most notably vitamin D3 and calcium—are necessary for bone structure, muscle control, eggshell formation, and the general well being of your lizards. The amount and the method of administration are less precisely agreed upon. If the supplement you choose contains phosphorus, check to make certain that the calcium:phosphorous ratio is 2:1.

A bearded dragon that lacks sufficient calcium in its diet is in trouble. In order to maintain the calcium level in the blood, the body will pull calcium from the bones. The bones become weakened and fragile. Rapidly growing baby bearded dragons and reproducing females require supplements with more frequency than dragons at other stages of their lives.

We have found the following guidelines to work well. Along with UVA/UVB lighting:

- We provide daily supplementation of D3 and calcium (actually we use a multivitamin—Osteoform) from hatching until the dragons are about one-quarter grown, then every second day until they are about one-half grown.

- We provide supplements about every fourth day when they are from one-half grown to when they are adult.

- We provide vitamin-mineral supplements to adult dragons weekly, but ovulating females who need extra calcium for eggshell formation are given supplements twice weekly.

The supplement may be blended into the prepared veggies and/or applied to crickets (the crickets are placed into a jar or bag with a little additive and shaken about until coated). Feed the insects to the lizards as soon after dusting as possible.

"Gut-loading" Food Insects

Unless they are continuously fed a diet of nutritious foods, insects will provide your lizards with little more than chitinous bulk. Feed all insects well for at least 24 hours before offering them to your beardeds. Several cricket diets that are high in calcium and vitamin D3 are now commercially available. Food insects will also eat many vegetables and cereals as well as lab-rodent chow. Provide a source of water or moisture from fruit such as apples, carrots, and oranges.

Water

Bearded dragons seem to metabolize much of their moisture requirements from the fresh plant material that they eat. However, they will also drink from a dish. In low-humidity areas, a shallow dish of fresh water may be kept with the bearded dragons at all times. In areas where high humidity prevails, to keep cage humidity as low as possible, it is better to offer your dragons water for a few hours every second day, after the dragons have warmed up and begun their daily behavioral regimen. Some breeders suggest, instead of providing a dish of water, you mist your beardeds heads daily, once their cage has warmed up.

A healthy, well-fed male bearded displays to a female.

Conditioning and Breeding Bearded Dragons

Although bearded dragons often breed well in captivity with little concerted preparation, some guidelines should be followed to ascertain their reproductive cycling.

Males, aggressive toward other males at all times, become savagely aggressive toward other male *Pogona* during the breeding season. To avoid problems, keep only a single male to one to three females in an indoor cage. Even in large outside cages, unless there are ample hiding spots and visual barriers, keeping more than a single male to a cage may affect not only your success at breeding but also the health of the males.

Sexing Your Dragon

It is difficult to impossible to reliably sex baby and juvenile bearded dragons. Sexual differences in adult dragons are present but are comparative and can be minimal.

Cycling

Under natural conditions, the life cycles of lizards are influenced by the seasonal climatic changes. Influencing factors include photoperiod, temperature, rainfall, and relative humidity. Even in captivity, certain of these cyclic stimuli can and should be approximated when preparing your dragons for breeding. All except rainfall seem

significant to the desert- and dry-savanna-dwelling bearded dragons.

The term *photoperiod* simply refers to the hours of daylight (as opposed to the hours of darkness) in any given day. Photoperiod is more seasonally variable at (or near) the poles than at the equator. The hours of daylight increase as winter gives way to spring and spring to summer and then decrease again in the autumn. Check the weather page in your local newspaper for the exact sunrise and sunset times, and periodically (about weekly) alter the numbers of hours that your cage is artificially illuminated. If you happen to be keeping your lizard in

Although usually placid, some inland bearded dragons will attempt to bite. The gaping mouth and distended beard tells you that this male has a bit of an attitude problem.

Adult male dragons often have:	Adult female dragons have:
A wider tail base (to accommodate the hemipenes) and wider cloacal opening	Narrower tail base and narrow cloacal opening
A broader, more strongly triangular head	Less strongly triangular head (narrower posteriorly)
Enlarged (but very irregularly placed and often darkened) femoral and preanal pores	Smaller and usually not darkened femoral pores
Darkened beards, especially during breeding season	Lighter colored beards
Less robust build	Heavy build (inordinately so when gravid)
Enhanced aggressive behavior (especially during breeding season)	Less aggressive; use circumduction (arm-waving) extensively

outside caging, allow Mother Nature to dictate photoperiod naturally. Of course, because they are a heliothermic species, brilliant illumination is necessary to induce peak activity in your dragons.

Temperatures, both daily and seasonal, can be altered with the prudent use of lights and/or heating elements. Bearded dragons are desert and dry-savanna lizards that are well adapted to hot summer temperatures and somewhat cooler winter ones. A drop of nighttime temperature is also permissible.

Not all dragon eggs are created equal. To produce healthy eggs that develop into robust hatchlings, your breeding bearded dragons must be in overall good health (it is better not to breed dragons in suboptimal health). Dragons seem to breed more reliably and to produce healthier eggs and hatchlings when they have undergone a 2-month-long period of winter cooling (not hibernation—just cooling!).

Generally speaking, in midwinter, you should provide the lowest humidity, the fewest hours of daylight, and the lowest nighttime temperatures. Ten hours of daylight should be the minimum. Allow the temperatures to cool to 80° F under the basking light, and to 60–65° F at night. Reduce the feeding, both in quantity at a given meal and in frequency. When temperatures again warm, increase meal size and frequency. Your lizards should be fed most heavily from early spring during the longest and warmest days of the year. Heavy springtime feedings are especially important for female dragons that need additional weight to enable them to breed.

Be sure to provide plenty of calcium and D3 throughout the year. These additives are especially important at the time of eggshell formation by adult female dragons and for proper bone development and the growth of hatchlings and juveniles.

Breeding

Courtship involves much body language by the male dragon, including beard distension, head-bobbing, body inflation, and circumduction. Male

Cycling will place bearded dragons of any color morphs into breeding readiness.

dragons usually restrict the escape of a receptive female by biting the back of the female's neck. During the height of the breeding season, this can cause open wounds that may need medical attention.

The Eggs

All bearded dragons are oviparous. That is, they reproduce by laying eggs. Their eggs have a pliable (and permeable) parchment-like shell. Depending on the species, a clutch may consist of from 6 to about 25 eggs; the smaller dragon species usually produce fewer eggs than the larger species.

Depending on the number of eggs she is carrying, a gravid female bearded dragon may look only reasonably heavy or may appear positively fat.

An adult female will usually produce four to six clutches a year (at 3- to 4-week intervals) for the first several years of her life. Unless she is in top-notch condition when she enters

the egging cycle, she can be quickly debilitated. Feed a reproducing female heavily on a nutritious diet between depositions.

The Deposition Site

In nature, female lizards carefully select the site that they instinctively feel will best suit the eggs for the approximately 60 days of incubation. Oviposition occurs during the hours of daylight, often in mid to late afternoon. Suitable laying sites must be provided for your gravid captive dragons. Bearded dragons of all species dig extensive nesting burrows. They dig the burrow with the forefeet, removing the loosened soil with the rear feet. When the female feels the hole is deep enough, she will reverse her position back in, and lay her eggs with only her nose showing. Following deposition, the burrow is methodically refilled. The main criterion for the selection of a nesting burrow seems to be that the

To restrain receptive females, male inland dragons bite the female on the nape.

species) to more than 12 in. (larger dragon species). The burrows may be dug laterally into the side of a provided pile of sandy loam or diagonally downward into the soil.

If a suitable nesting site is not provided, dragons (and most other oviparous reptiles) may retain the eggs until natural deposition is difficult or impossible. At that point in time, veterinary intervention is needed to administer a hormonal stimulant or to remove the eggs surgically.

The eggs of smaller dragon species may take only 42 days to incubate, whereas those of the larger forms may occasionally take 80 or more days.

In some cases, especially where suitable deposition sites are difficult to find, females may nest communally. The eggs of a given clutch often all hatch on the same day, but occasionally several days are involved.

soil is soft enough to be worked with relative ease and is of a consistency that the burrow retains its shape while being dug. If an obstruction is encountered while digging, the female will often leave the site, choose another, and begin over. A nesting burrow may be 5 in. in length (smaller dragon

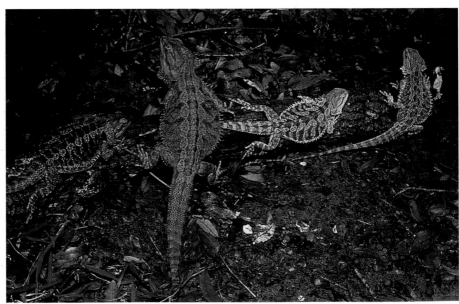

The female Red flame dragon (far left), when bred with the male Sandfire, produced young similar in coloration to the two 8-month-olds on the right.

Egg Incubation— An Overview

Following deposition, remove the eggs as soon as possible for incubation. It seems best, but may not be as critical as we once thought, if the orientation in which the egg was found is not changed. (In other words, just to be safe, keep the same side up.) Infertile eggs may be present in any given clutch. Additionally, a certain percentage of embryonic mortality should be expected.

Perlite and vermiculite have proven to be ideal incubation media. Moisten whichever you choose to use with four parts of water to five or six parts of the dry perlite or vermiculite (by volume). It should be moist enough to clump when squeezed but should not drip water. Place 1–1.5 in. of the moistened medium in the bottom of a plastic shoe box. The eggs of bearded dragons seem to incubate most successfully if they are one-half to two-thirds buried in the substrate. Simply make a depression for each egg with a fingertip. Once the eggs are in place, put the lid on the shoe box and put it in the incubator. A shallow open dish of water in the incubator will help keep the relative humidity high.

If the medium is too dry or too wet, the permeable eggshells of bearded dragons readily allow desiccation or overhydration of the eggs. Either can cause the death of the embryo. Watch the eggs closely during incubation. If the eggs begin to collapse, increase the moisture slightly; if they get turgid and slick, decrease the moisture. Do note, however, that even

Your own selective breeding can allow you to choose red, orange, or yellow coloration.

under ideal incubation conditions, when full-term is neared, dimpling and a concurrent lack of eggshell turgidity is normal. Some eggs may go full-term but, if the embryo is weak, fail to hatch. Some of these babies may be saved by carefully slitting the

The female bearded needs dampened soil so she can dig the chamber for her eggs.

Scrape with the right foot, then scrape with the left foot. A female bearded carefully digs her nest.

eggshell. If the baby within is viable, it may emerge within a day or two, but, even with extra care, weak hatchlings often succumb within a few days following emergence.

The sex of many lizard species is determined by the temperature at which the egg is incubated. This is called temperature-dependent sex determination. This does not seem to be true with bearded dragons. Both males and females are produced at all suitable incubation temperatures. Bearded dragons will hatch successfully at incubator temperatures between 81 and 85° F; 83–84° F is optimal.

What you'd like to see, some 40-plus days after deposition: baby beardeds emerging from the eggs.

Making Your Own Incubator

The following materials are needed for one incubator:

- 1 wafer thermostat (obtainable from feed stores; these are commonly used in incubators for chicks)
- 1 thermometer
- 1 Styrofoam cooler—one with thick sides (a fish-shipping box is ideal)
- 1 heat tape
- 1 electrical cord and wall plug
- 3 wire nuts
- 1 piece of 1 × 2 in. mesh hardware cloth, large enough for a u-shaped shelf

Poke a hole through the lid of the Styrofoam cooler and suspend the thermostat from the inside. The temperature adjustment handle of the thermostat should protrude through the lid and be easily worked without opening the incubator. The two wires should be inside. Add another hole through the lid for a thermometer so that you can check on the inside temperature without opening the top. If there's no flange on the thermometer to keep it from slipping through the hole in the lid, wind a rubber band around the thermometer several times to form a flange.

Your goal is to wire the thermostat between the heat tape and the electrical cord in order to regulate the amount of heat produced by the heat tape.

Cut the electrical cord off the heat tape, leaving about 18 in. of the cord on the heat tape. Make a hole through the side of the Styrofoam box, about 5 in. below the top edge. Pull the electrical cord through the hole, leaving the plug end outside (don't plug it in just yet!). Strip off about a half-inch of the insulation from the wiring at the cut end, and separate the two wires for a few inches.

Coil the heat tape loosely in the bottom of the Styrofoam box, making sure that it doesn't cross over itself at any point. Coil the tape so the recently cut end is near the electrical cord. Strip off about a half-inch of the insulation from the end of the wiring, and separate the two wires for a few inches.

Using one of the wire nuts, connect one of the red wires of the thermostat to one of the electrical wires of the heat tape. Use a second nut to connect the second red wire of the thermostat to one of the wires of the electrical cord. The third nut is used to connect the second wire of the electrical cord to the second wire of the heat tape (in effect, reestablishing part of the original wiring between the heat tape and its electrical cord).

That's all there is to it. Put the lid on the cooler and plug in the thermostat/heater. Wait half an

Homemade incubator.

A few days before hatching, the viable eggs will begin to look as if they are collapsing. This is actually a good sign at this point—soon small bearded lizards will emerge.

hour and check the temperature. The L-shaped pin on the top of the thermostat is the rheostat; turn it to increase or decrease the temperature inside your new incubator. You want the inside to be 80–86°F.

Once you have the temperature regulated, add your hardware cloth "shelf" and put the container of eggs atop the shelf. Close the egg container.

You can buy a commercial incubator—just make sure the thermostat is adjustable. Some breeders use cabinets and a 100-watt bulb to provide the necessary warmth.

Check the temperature daily and add a little water to the incubating medium if it gets dry (it should stay damp enough to stick together when you stick your finger into it, or when you push it into a little heap with your finger). Take care to add the water to the medium, not onto the eggs. The preferred humidity is 100 percent. Placing an open deli container, half-filled with water, onto the hardware cloth shelf will also help maintain the humidity.

How do you know if the eggs are fertile? By the end of the first week, those eggs that are not fertile will turn yellow, harden, and begin to collapse. Remove and discard them. Those that are fertile will remain white and turgid to the touch.

At the end of the incubation period—which may be as little as 42 days for some species but is usually 60, 70, or even 80 days for inland bearded dragons—the babies will cut a slit in their egg with an egg tooth on the tip of their snout.

After pipping, the babies will remain in the eggs from several hours to more than a day. After hatching, they should be removed to another terrarium and, once active, offered food, a sunning spot, and water. They should shed within a few days.

Care of the Young

In the wild, baby bearded dragons emerging from a nest would quickly scatter far and wide. They are seldom able to do so in captivity.

Typically, baby dragons are grouped, a dozen or more to a plastic blanket box set up with a paper towel substrate, basking areas, and hiding areas. Anthropomorphically, there is

Hatchling beardeds are 4–5 inches long, but should be voracious feeders in a day or two. No reputable breeder will sell them before they are six inches long, and proven feeders.

hardly anything cuter than a group of hatchling bearded dragons, scrambling over each other to partake of the hot spots, to reach fresh food, or to ascend to the highest point in their cage. But cute, in this case, equates to stress. Numbers of baby dragons in a cage can cause overt aggression, biting, and has been associated with stress-related proliferation of endoparasites, which, in turn, cause digestive problems. We suggest that dragons be sized in the largest cages possible, that they be carefully watched for aggressive behavior (and segregated when necessary), and that the cause of any loose and sticky stools be immediately addressed.

Despite these problems and the fact that hatchling and juvenile bearded dragons can be aggressive enough to cause injury to each other, if you watch them closely, they can be successfully reared in groups. To prevent overt aggression, it is important to keep all baby dragons in any given group approximately the same size, to remove the most aggressive ones, and to keep the babies very well fed. A well-fed baby dragon will be less inclined to nip and injure the toes and tailtips of its cage mates—even those of similar size. Severed tailtips or toes will not regenerate.

By placing the fastest growing, largest, and most aggressive babies into their own size groups and by feeding heavily, the potential for many problems will be considerably lessened.

A Note on Feeding Baby Bearded Dragons

Hatchling bearded dragons of all species have surprisingly robust appetites. We feel that it is important that they are fed a minimum of once daily, and that twice or three times daily is better. Baby bearded dragons will attempt to eat prey items that are far too large for their well being. A meal of several small crickets, mealworms, and mixed veggies is far better (and safer) for baby dragons than a meal consisting of a single large insect. They will swallow large insects, but this isn't a good idea. Several hours following the eating of a proportionately large prey item, baby dragons (and adults, too) have occasionally undergone convulsions and partial paralysis that has usually resulted in the death of the dragon.

Be safe. Provide more frequent feedings of smaller prey.

Health

Sometimes a health "shift" is only temporary—if your bearded seems a bit listless, and not interested in feeding, wait a few days. Beardeds often stop feeding when they get close to shedding time. Then they shed, and they may look a bit moth-eaten in the process. They will then again show interest in food, be ready to climb onto your hand, and start to check out their surroundings to be sure another bearded has not wandered by looking to take over the best basking spot.

Endoparasites

The presence of internal parasites in lizards from the wild is a foregone conclusion. However, few hobbyists realize that captive-bred and hatched lizards may also harbor endoparasites and other pathogens. *Pseudomonas*, coccidia, roundworms, pinworms, nematodes, tapeworms, and/or parasitic protozoans are typical endoparasites.

Endoparasites can be diagnosed by fecal exams. Whether or not your veterinarian treats your lizard for endoparasites may depend on the behavior and condition of the lizard. Certainly the problems created by endoparasitic loads in weakened lizards need to be addressed promptly. However, if the specimen in question is bright-eyed, alert, and feeding well and has a good color, you and your vet may agree to forego treating the animal. Endoparasitic loads can actually diminish if you keep the cage of your specimen scrupulously clean, thereby preventing reinfestation.

Getting rid of endoparasites means administering a substance that is toxic to the parasites in dosages that will not harm your lizard. Obviously, dosages must be accurate, which is why you need to take your animal to your veterinarian. To begin with, your veterinarian can accurately weigh your lizard, whose weight determines the dosage of medication to be used. It is also very easy for a layperson to miscalculate metric conversions or to fail to actually get the correct dosage into the lizard. The result may be fatal or futile. Let your reptile veterinarian do the work for which he or she was trained. So that you may discuss possible endoparasitic treatments with your veterinarian, some sample treatments and dosages appear at the end of this chapter.

Coccidia

The presence of coccidia in dragons' guts is an insidious and persistent problem. An overabundance of these protozoans can impair digestion and cause your dragon to be listless and run down. Coccidia can, though direct and secondary infections, cause death. Bearded dragons have their very own species of coccidium, *Isospora amphiboluri*. Because these parasites do not require an outside host to complete their life cycle, immense numbers can quickly build up. If your dragon is

Now I'm calm, now I'm not. An adult male coastal bearded dragon looks at the photographer and flares out his beard—and looks very fierce in the process.

dull-eyed and listless and has loose or smelly stools that stick to the anal opening, coccidia (or other endoparasites) should be suspected, and a veterinary assessment performed.

Ectoparasites

External parasites are less problematic to treat than endoparasites. With captive-born beardeds you should never see ticks or mites. Both are easily dealt with. Ticks, which are deflated and seedlike when empty but rounded and bladderlike when engorged, may be removed manually. They embed their mouthparts deeply when feeding, and if merely pulled from the lizard, these may break off in the wound. It is best to dust them individually with Sevin powder first and then to return a few minutes later and twist the ticks off gently with a pair of dog-tick tweezers. Mites may be combatted with Sevin dust (best in arid climates) or with Ivomectin mist. Total eradication of mites will take two or more treatments at 9-day intervals. These treatments have the potential of being debilitating or fatal to hatchling dragons. Seek the services of a reptile-oriented vet, especially when treating young *Pogona*.

Metabolic Bone Disease

The technical names for metabolic bone disease (MBD) are nutritional secondary hyperthyroidism and fibrous osteodystrophy. In simplified terms, MBD is the result of too little calcium in the diet and not enough vitamin D3, the vitamin that enables the body to utilize calcium. In dragons, MBD's basic symptoms are the inability to walk, spastic twitching of the extended limbs, foreshortened and softened jawbones, and swollen, pliable limbs. Left untreated, your animal will die.

To exist, a dragon needs a certain level of calcium in the blood. When the level of blood calcium drops below a certain percentage, the parathyroid glands then begin drawing calcium out of the bones and moving that calcium to the bloodstream to maintain the levels there. As the bones lose their rigidity, parts of them become overlaid with a fibrous tissue to compensate for the loss of strength—hence the swollen, "chubby" look to the face and the limbs. Poor dragon! No dragon deserves this.

The bones are very easily broken at this point. In its early stages, MBD is treatable. UVA/UVB lighting and vita-min–mineral supplements are crucial; veterinary assessment is mandatory.

Respiratory Ailments

Well-acclimated, properly maintained bearded dragons are not prone to res-piratory ailments. But if they are stressed, or only marginally healthy and are subjected to unnatural peri-ods of cold (especially damp cold), bearded may occasionally break down with colds or pneumonia. Some respi-ratory ailments may also be associated with the weakening brought about by a heavy endoparasite burden.

Respiratory ailments are indicated by sneezing, lethargic demeanor, and unnaturally rapid, often shallow, breathing. As the disease progresses, rasping and bubbling may accompany each of your lizard's breaths. At this stage, the respiratory ailment is often critical and can be fatal.

Begin by separating the ill lizard from any cage mates, placing it in its own cage, and then elevating the illu-minated basking area (NOT the entire cage) to about 110° F. The more opti-mal its surroundings, the better able the specimen is to deal with a respira-tory ailment.

The rest of the cage should be maintained at 85–90° F. If the symp-toms of respiratory distress do not greatly lessen within a day or two, do not delay any longer. Call your veteri-narian, and take your lizard to him or her for antibiotic treatment.

There are many "safe" drugs avail-able, but some respiratory ailments do not respond well to these. The newer aminoglycoside drugs, and others, newer still, are more effective, but they are correspondingly more dangerous. There is little latitude in dosage amounts, and the lizard must be well hydrated to ensure against renal (kid-ney) damage. The injection site for aminoglycosides should be between the front legs and midbody to avoid damaging the kidneys.

Other Maladies

Several other diseases and maladies may occur rarely. Among these are:

- Mineralization of internal organs: This is caused by the overmetabo-lization of calcium and is known as hypercalcemia. A treatment has now been developed but is both lengthy and expensive. Treatment requires about 2 weeks of monitoring by a veterinarian. There is a fine line between too much and not enough calcium and vitamin D3. Once diag-nosed and corrected, you'll need to reduce both calcium and D3 intake by your specimen. If untreated or too far advanced, overdosing sup-plements can be fatal.

- Hypoglycemia: This relates to low blood sugar. Stress or pancreatic dysfunction can be the causative agent. The stress factor is correctable; the pancreatic dysfunction, most commonly caused by an insulin-secreting tumor, usually is not.
- Hindquarter paralysis: See MBD symptoms, page 39, and too-large food items, page 26.

Medical Treatments for Internal Parasites

Because of the complexities of identification of endoparasites and the need to weigh specimens for them to be treated accurately, the eradication of internal parasites is best left to a qualified reptile veterinarian. These are a few of the recommended medications and dosages.

Amoebas and Trichomonads

For amoebas and trichomonads, a singular treatment of 40–50 mg/kg of metronidazole is given orally. The treatment is repeated in 2 weeks. Dimetridazole can also be used, but the dosage is very different. For 5 days, 40–50 mg/kg of dimetrizadole is administered daily. The treatment is then repeated in 2 weeks. All treatments with both medications are administered once daily.

Coccidia

Many treatments are available. The dosages of sulfadiazine, sulfamerazine, and sulfamethazine are identical. Administer 75 mg/kg the first day, then follow up for the next 5 days with 45 mg/kg. All treatments are administered orally and once daily. Sulfadimethoxine is also effective. The initial dosage is 90 mg/kg orally to be followed on the next 5 days with 45 mg/kg orally. All dosages are administered once daily. Trimethoprim-sulfa may also be used by administering 30 mg/kg once daily for 7 days.

Cestodes (Tapeworms)

Several effective treatments are available. Bunamidine may be administered orally at a dosage of 50 mg/kg. A second treatment occurs in 14 days. Niclosamide, given orally at a dosage of 150 mg/kg, is also effective. A second treatment is given in 2 weeks. Finally, praziquantel may be administered either orally or intramuscularly. The dosage is 5–8 mg/kg and is to be repeated in 14 days.

Trematodes (Flukes)

Praziquantel at 8 mg/kg may be administered either orally or intramuscularly. The treatment is repeated in 2 weeks.

Nematodes (Roundworms)

Several effective treatments are available. Levamisole, an injectable intraperitoneal treatment, should be administered at a dosage of 10 mg/kg, and the treatment should be repeated in 2 weeks. Ivermectin, injected intramuscularly in a dosage of 200 mg/kg, is effective. The treatment is to be repeated in 2 weeks. Ivermectin can be toxic to certain taxa. Thiabendazole and fenbendazole have similar dosages. Both are administered orally at 50–100 mg/kg and repeated in 14 days. Mebendazole is administered orally at a dosage of 20–25 mg/kg and is repeated in 14 days.

Special Interest Groups

Herpetological Societies

Reptile and amphibian enthusiasts can meet like-minded people and learn more about their hobby through herp societies, monthly magazines, and professional associations, in addition to commercial functions such as herp expos.

Herpetological societies (or clubs) exist in major cities in North America, Europe, and other areas of the world. Most have monthly meetings, some publish newsletters, and many host or sponsor field trips or picnics, or indulge in various other interactive functions. Among the members are enthusiasts of varying expertise. Information about these clubs can often be found by querying pet shop employees, high school science teachers,

university biology department professors, or curators or employees at the department of herpetology at local museums and zoos. All such clubs welcome inquiries and new members.

Two of the professional herpetological societies are:

Society for the Study of Amphibians and Reptiles (SSAR)
Department of Zoology
Miami University
Oxford, OH 45056

Herpetologist's League
c/o Texas National Heritage Program
Texas Parks and Wildlife Department
4200 Smith School Road
Austin, TX 78744

The SSAR publishes two quarterly journals: *Herpetological Review*, which contains husbandry, range extensions, news on ongoing field studies, and the like, and *Journal of Herpetology*, which contains articles more oriented toward academic herpetology.

There is one hobbyist magazine that publishes articles on all aspects of herpetology and herpetoculture (including lizards):

Reptiles
P O Box 6050
Mission Viejo, CA 92690

The Web provides both good and bad information. Simply type "bearded dragons," or ask specifically about a topic, such as "bearded dragon diet."

Glossary

Ambient temperature: The temperature of the surrounding environment.

Anterior: Toward the front.

Anus: The external opening of the cloaca; the vent.

Caudal: Pertaining to the tail.

Circumduction: The stylized waving of a forelimb as a gesture of appeasement.

Cloaca: The common chamber into which digestive, urinary, and reproductive systems empty and which itself opens exteriorly through the vent or anus.

Deposition: As used here, the laying of the eggs.

Deposition site: The spot chosen by the female to lay her eggs.

Diurnal: Active by day.

Dorsal: Pertaining to the back; upper surface.

Dorsolateral: Pertaining to the upper sides.

Dorsum: The upper surface.

Femoral pores: Enlarged, pheromone-emitting scales on the underside of the femur.

Genus: A taxonomic classification of a group of species having similar characteristics. The genus falls between the next higher designation of family and the next lower designation of species.

Genera is the plural of genus. The generic name is always capitalized when written.

Gravid: The reptilian equivalent of mammalian pregnancy.

Heliothermic: A species that basks in the sunlight to attain thermal optimums.

Hemipenes: The dual copulatory organs of male lizards and snakes.

Hemipenis: The singular form of hemipenes.

Juvenile: A young or immature specimen.

Lateral: Pertaining to the side.

Middorsal: Pertaining to the middle of the back.

Midventral: Pertaining to the center of the belly or abdomen.

Oviparous: Reproducing by means of eggs that hatch after laying.

Poikilothermic: A species with no internal body temperature regulation. The old term was *cold-blooded*.

Posterior: Toward the rear.

Preanal pores: A series of pores, often in the shape of an anteriorly directed chevron, located anterior to the anus.

Saxicolous: Rock-dwelling.

Serrate: Sawlike.

Species: A group of similar creatures that produce viable young when breeding. The taxonomic designation that falls beneath genus and above subspecies.

Subcaudal: Beneath the tail.

Subdigital: Beneath the toes.

Subspecies: The subdivision of a species. A race that may differ slightly in color, size, scalation, or other criteria.

Because they are large, heavy-bodied, and relatively slow moving, bearded dragons are of interest to many hobbyists.

Terrestrial: Land-dwelling.
Thermoregulate: To regulate (body) temperature by choosing a warmer or cooler environment.
Tympanum: The external eardrum.
Vent: The external opening of the cloaca; the anus.

Venter: The underside of a creature; the belly.
Ventral: Pertaining to the undersurface or belly.
Ventrolateral: Pertaining to the sides of the venter (belly).

Note: Other scientific definitions are contained in the following two volumes:

Peters, James A. 1964. *Dictionary of Herpetology*. New York: Hafner Publishing Co.

Wareham, David C. 1993. *The Reptile and Amphibian Keeper's Dictionary*. London: Blandford.

No matter its size, a healthy bearded dragon has bright eyes and an alert demeanor.

Index

Note: Bold indicates photo captions.